JEFF GORDON

Rewriting the Record Book

by

Ken Garfield

SPORTS PUBLISHING INC.
www.SportsPublishingInc.com

Series editor: Mike Persinger
Production manager: Erin J. Sands
Cover design: Julie L. Denzer
Developmental editor: Claudia Mitroi
Photo editor: Sandy Arneson
Photos: *The Charlotte Observer*

ISBN: 1-58382-055-8
Library of Congress Catalog Card Number: 99-69770
SPORTS PUBLISHING INC.
www.SportsPublishingInc.com

Printed in the United States.

To the fans, the ones who really make the men of NASCAR go.

*Jeff raises his fist into the air after winning the 1998
ACDelco 400 and the Winston Cup Points
Championship. (Charlotte Observer/Jeff Siner)*

Contents

Acknowledgments

No one can bring an athlete like Jeff Gordon to life without a lot of help, so thanks goes out to Tom Bast and all the good folks at Sports Publishing Inc. Their love for games and the people who play them sure does entertain a lot of fans.

Thanks to Charlotte Observer deputy sports editor Mike Persinger and the newspaper's NASCAR team—David Poole, Jim Utter and columnist Scott Fowler—for taking readers racing each and every weekend. No newspaper does it better.

Appreciation goes to Lowe's Motor Speedway's Humpy Wheeler and Jerry Gappens and longtime NASCAR sportswriters Bob Myers and Tom Higgins (a true NASCAR journalism legend!) for giving us glimpses of Jeff on and off the track. Race caps off to the Jeff Gordon team for its help as well.

Thanks to the good people at Calvary Church

and Motor Racing Outreach in Charlotte, whose wonderful ministry allows Jeff to reach so many people in the world away from the speedways.

Thanks to the millions of fans who hang on every race, from Rockingham to Darlington to Watkins Glen clear to Sears Point, Calif. They boo, they cheer, they wear their favorite driver's colors with pride. When all is said and done, they are the ones who combine with Jeff and the rest of the drivers to make NASCAR America's most colorful spectator sport.

Finally, a great big thanks to my wife, Sharon, and daughter, Ellen, for allowing me to be such a crazy fan of all sports. And thanks to our son, Matthew, for being there with me every step of the way, live and via television.

We've cheered ourselves hoarse and happy, haven't we?

Jeff stands next to his car, enjoying a laugh with friends, prior to the running of the 1998 ACDelco 400 at North Carolina Speedway. (Charlotte Observer/Jeff Siner)

Mention some of the greatest American athletes of today's generation and you'd have to start with Tiger Woods, Ken Griffey Jr., Peyton Manning and Michael Jordan, even if he is retired. No list of superstars, though, would be complete without the name of a fresh-faced young man from Indiana who has taken the world of NASCAR by storm.

Jeff Gordon is a superstar who is making all the right moves on and off the track.

Racing one kind of car or another since he was a boy in small-town Indiana, Jeff has become one of the biggest names in racing. Since breaking into NASCAR in 1993, he has gone on to win three Winston Cup points championships, 49 races and more than $31 million on the biggest, most competitive stock car racing circuit in the world.

A sports magazine, in fact, named him the fifth greatest NASCAR driver of the entire 20th Century.

But it's not just winning races from Charlotte (N.C.) to Daytona (Fla.) to Darlington (S.C.) to Sears Point (Calif.) that has won Jeff so much acclaim everywhere he goes. It's the way he carries himself as a wholesome example for young race fans —signing autographs, appearing at charity events and expressing his strong religious faith to youth groups throughout America. He's a real celebrity, appearing on national TV talk shows. Some people even say he looks a little like movie star Tom Cruise!

The day before NBC-TV televised its first NASCAR race from Homestead, Fla., it presented a show on Saturday afternoon introducing America to the sport. The host for the show? Jeff Gordon!

NASCAR superstar Dale Earnhardt used to

kiddingly call Jeff "Wonder Boy," more out of respect than anything else. "He's the best young talent that's ever been out there," the so-called Man in Black told The Charlotte Observer in 1995.

Humpy Wheeler, president of Lowe's Motor Speedway in Charlotte, is one of the most respected men in the sport. Wheeler says Gordon is a lot like the great NFL quarterbacks who started out in youth football. Jeff slid behind the wheel of a car as a young boy. "He started out when he was six," Wheeler says . . . "He kept on moving up and up and up, excelling like a pee wee quarterback in Pop Warner youth football . . ."

Jerry Gappens of Lowe's Motor Speedway talks about Jeff's courage behind the wheel of his Chevy Monte Carlo, how he's willing to drive just a little harder into the turns than his competitors. How his hand-eye coordination allows him to avoid wrecks that might take out a lesser driver on the

Jeff (left) is congratulated by car owner Rick Hendrick after winning the pole for the 1993 Mello Yello 500 at Charlotte Motor Speedway. (Charlotte Observer/Mark B. Sluder)

short tracks, road courses and superspeedways that make up the NASCAR circuit. And how his ability to cooperate so smoothly with his crew chief and his famed Rainbow Warriors pit crew gives him that little extra edge.

"He's got nerve," Gappens says. "He's certainly braver than the average human being."

But it's not just Jeff's courage and ability to maneuver his No. 24 Chevrolet at 200 mph that Gappens admires.

It's how Jeff stops to sign autographs for as long as it takes. How he talks publicly about the importance of his family, especially his wife, Brooke, who travels with him to every race. And how he broke down and cried when he won his first race, the Coca-Cola 600, in May 1994 in Charlotte.

To Gappens, Jeff is someone to look up to: "He's a great role model. He's got the clean-cut look about him. He has the ability to relate well to kids.

People can walk up to him and say something easier than they could to Dale Earnhardt or Lawrence Taylor.

"He has the natural ability to make you feel good about the two or three minutes you get with him," Gappens said.

And what does Jeff have to say about who really deserves the credit for his success?

"The first thing I want to do when I get out of the car is to give God the glory," Jeff said one evening during a NASCAR program at Calvary Church in Charlotte, N.C. "I'm not out there doing it by myself."

Since it began in Daytona Beach in 1947, NASCAR has grown to become one of America's hottest sports. Each season's 34 races at 21 tracks from New York to California draw six million fans in person and another 112 million who watch on TV. NASCAR recently signed a deal with Fox, NBC and Turner Sports to televise the races—a deal that is expected to bring NASCAR some $2.8 billion. Some races at the biggest, fastest tracks – at Daytona or Charlotte, for example—draw 200,000 fans in one heart-stopping night or day. Fans spend some $2 billion a year on race tickets, clothing and other souvenirs. The top 17 sports events in America in terms of live attendance each year are usually NASCAR races.

As you'll learn in the pages to follow, a lot of the credit for NASCAR's popularity has to go to a talented 28-year-old who doesn't smoke or drink, who reads the Bible and who credits hard work and teamwork for his success.

Jeff Gordon has taken the race world by storm.

Jeff blurs past the fans in the front stretch of North Carolina Speedway on his way to victory in the 1998 GM Goodwrench Service Plus 400. (The Charlotte Observer/Jeff Siner)

CHAPTER ONE

Born to Race

One of the world's greatest race car drivers started going fast like most kids do—on his BMX bicycle at age 4, racing other youngsters around the block in Vallejo, Calif.

He was just a little guy, 30 pounds or so, but even at that size and age, his mother, Carol, and his stepfather, John Bickford, could see the gleam in his eye and the determination in his heart. He had to be going fast!

Jeff soon moved up from bicycles to quarter midget race cars—his parents hoped they would be

Jeff's crew goes to work on the car on the final pit stop of the 1998 Brickyard 400 race at the Indianapolis Motor Speedway. (Charlotte Observer/Patrick Schneider)

safer than a bike. John Bickford would take Jeff out to a nearby fairground and let him get the feel of handling a car with an engine not much bigger than a lawn mower's on a track cut from a grassy field.

"We'd take that car out every night after I got home from work and run it lap after lap," Bickford says. "Jeff couldn't seem to get enough of it."

Bickford was in the auto parts business, so he knew his way around race cars. It wasn't long before Jeff really started zooming around the track.

As a youngster, Jeff was taught a great lesson: to win, you had to finish. When he was six, his stepdad made him obey a no-contact rule—Jeff had to give back the winner's trophy if he bumped another car. And he had to do it without crying!

Jeff won his first national championship in 1979, in the quarter midget division. He was just eight years old. He competed in quartet midgets and go-karts. By the time he turned 12, he was racing 150 times a year.

Bickford and Jeff both remember those early days with a lot of happiness.

Bickford said he worked on developing Jeff's ability to tune everything out, and just keep his concentration on the car and the track. "Jeff had superb hand-eye coordination, learned rapidly and developed a rhythm. We worked on all of that. He became like watching music."

Jeff said all the credit for whatever he has done in racing should go to his parents for their support, patience and enthusiasm for showing him how to race.

The Bickfords moved in 1986 from California to Pittsboro, Ind., a friendly little town of about 1,000 people, 20 miles west of Indianapolis.

The reason?

So the family could be closer to Midwestern tracks where Jeff could race sprint cars and there was no minimum age requirement.

Jerry Gappens, who works at Lowe's Motor Speedway, knows about Jeff's heroics as a youngster in Indiana—Gappens' parents ran a dirt track in Terre Haute, Ind., and Jeff used to race there.

Gappens appreciates how hard Jeff worked to become the youngest Winston Cup champion of the modern era in 1995, at age 24. "People don't realize he's been working at this since he was four years old," Gappens said.

One track owner says he'll never forget one move Jeff made one night: "Once I saw him make a move to pass someone on the back stretch. He ran on the back wheels of another car, came down, took the lead and never missed a beat. We still use that piece on our midget car advertising."

Jeff was a well-behaved student at Tri-West High School in Pittsboro. Folks still remember him coming downtown to Frank and Mary's restaurant, where he'd dig into their apple pie a la mode. But

Jeff enjoys a laugh with crew chief Ray Evernham in the garage area at Daytona International Speedway in 1999. (Charlotte Observer/Jeff Siner)

mostly what they remember about Jeff was how he raced and how he won.

In all, Jeff won more than 100 sprint car races as a high schooler. The cars generally weighed about 1,300 pounds and had a 650-horsepower engine. He finished fourth in a race on the night of his high school graduation.

His life was all about cars, and Jeff doesn't regret that it cost him some time to do the things other teen-agers do.

"I never really had much of a best friend," he says. "Most of my time was spent racing, so I did miss out on some of the things the other kids did. But I never have regretted it."

Neither have the folks back home in Pittsboro, where Jeff is treated as the Great American Hero he is.

He returned to his hometown in the summer of 1999 when they named part of County Road

275 after him—Jeff Gordon Boulevard. The Gingham Goose gift shop on Main Street carries Jeff Gordon beanie babies, toboggans, craft items, baby shoes, cups, hats, even wallpaper trim. Saleswoman Charlene Alexander says she's not much of a NASCAR fan.

"I'm just a Jeff Gordon fan," she squeals.

And she sure doesn't like it when fans of Dale Earnhardt, Dale Jarrett, Tony Stewart and other drivers boo their favorite son. Front-runners get their share of boos in most sports, especially NASCAR, where the underdog is taken to many fans' hearts.

"I don't think a lot of them treat Jeff Gordon right," Alexander says. "I think he's a good Christian. He never forgets to thank the Lord."

Having won bicycle races, quarter midget races, go-kart races and then sprint car races on the U.S. Automobile Club circuit, there was still another great big world for Jeff to conquer.

The greatest chapter in his racing life began one summer morning in 1990. His parents had started talking to him about NASCAR, and Jeff decided to explore this fast world of full-bodied cars by attending a driving school run by former NASCAR star Buck Baker in Rockingham, N.C., about two hours east of Charlotte in the beautiful Sandhills of North Carolina. He had grown up watching the Indianapolis 500, dreaming of one day racing those kinds of cars on the world's most famous track. But as soon as he slid behind the wheel of a stock car that day in North Carolina and started to get the hang of it, he was hooked—for life!

Here on the track at N.C. Motor Speedway was where Jeff discovered the car he would learn to master. Here was where his life was about to take a great new shape.

"That first day," he told *Sports Illustrated*, "the

Jeff returns to the garage a winner after speeding to the pole in qualifying for the 1994 Coca-Cola 600 in Charlotte. (Charlotte Observer/Mark Sluder)

first time I got in a (stock) car, I said, 'This is it. This is what I want to do.' The car was different from anything that I was used to. It was so big and heavy. It felt very fast but very smooth. I loved it."

It wasn't long before the drivers of NASCAR were going to have to make room for a new superstar on the speedway.

Jeff gives the "OK" sign as he climbs from his No. 24 Chevrolet after securing the pole position for the 1997 Coca Cola 600 in Charlotte. (Charlotte Observer/Christopher A. Record)

2

Tears in His Eyes

It was a call they made as a team: Should they gamble by putting on two tires during the last pit stop of the Coca-Cola 600 at Charlotte, N.C.? Or should they play it safe and put on four tires?

Jeff Gordon, crew chief Ray Evernham and the Rainbow Warriors team went with the risky but the right decision that record-setting afternoon of May 29, 1994, in front of a packed house at one of NASCAR's most famous tracks. They put on two

Jeff and his crew celebrate a win with champagne. (Charlotte Observer/Jeff Siner)

tires, got out of the pits nine seconds faster than Rusty Wallace and sealed the first win in a career that would see a lot more wins—and soon.

But the daring move isn't all that NASCAR fans remember from that special day. They remember what Jeff did when he realized he was going to get his very first victory on the super-fast, super-competitive Winston Cup circuit.

He cried like a baby.

"This is the highest feeling in the world," he said after climbing from his No. 24 Chevy with the eye-catching rainbow paint scheme. "If there's a higher feeling than this, I don't know what it is. Those last few laps, I was just trying to keep from hitting the wall because of all the tears in my face. The white-flag lap (the last one), I choked up and completely lost it."

Jerry Gappens of Lowe's Motor Speedway in Charlotte remembers Jeff's tears with admiration.

"His emotion is something I appreciate," Gappens said. "You don't see a lot of men share their emotion."

Jeff's tears that Sunday afternoon in Charlotte have become a real legend in racing. At the NASCAR awards banquet in New York City, he kidded Dale Earnhardt about it. "I know, Earnhardt," Jeff joked from the podium during his champion's speech, all dressed up for the black-tie affair that is televised live each year. "Real men don't cry."

The tears were as surprising as the way the race ended that day in Charlotte.

Wallace, a fierce competitor in his No. 2 Ford, looked like a sure thing for Victory Lane. He came in for a pit stop on Lap 375, with just 25 laps to go. He took on four tires in 17.22 seconds. But Jeff outfoxed him, coming in on Lap 381 and taking on two tires on the right side of his car in just 8.65

seconds. He was hoping that his car would still grip the track with only two fresh tires instead of four new ones.

The car did grip. And in the split-second world of NASCAR, those few seconds he saved putting on just two tires were enough to give Jeff the lead when Ricky Rudd stopped for gas on Lap 390.

When a car can travel the length of a football field (300 feet) in a split second, you can imagine how every decision can affect the outcome of a NASCAR race.

Rusty Wallace was impressed with the youngster who beat him that day: "I never thought he'd try two tires," he told reporters, "and I never thought it'd work. It was a chancy move. It was a pretty savvy move on their part."

The victory was all the proof that team owner Rick Hendrick, an auto dealer from Charlotte, needed to know he had landed a superstar in the

NASCAR fans hang their hopes and their clipboards on a string as they wait for Jeff to pass by. (Charlotte Observer/Patrick Schneider)

making when he signed Jeff to his Hendrick Motorsports race team in 1992.

Hendrick, one of the nation's biggest car dealers, knew about Jeff's lifetime of racing from bicycles on up, and how Jeff had moved from California to Indiana to get more chances to compete. He had heard about Jeff's reputation. He watched him race in Atlanta that year. He loved what he saw in this young, handsome daredevil who would become the thoroughbred of his racing stable that also includes another superstar, Terry Labonte.

"He was on the ragged edge all day," Hendrick said. "There was this haze coming off his tires. Other than Tim Richmond (a driver who died in 1989 at age 34), I had never seen anything like him."

Jeff's victory came in his 41st start, and it won him and the team $200,000. But more than that it opened the sports world's eyes, that here was a driver who was ready to start making his mark.

Jeff celebrates wining the 1994 Coca-Cola 600 with his crew chief. (Charlotte Observer/Christopher A. Record)

The sports world's eyes opened even wider on Aug. 6, 1994. That's the day Jeff won his second race, in what is considered by many the most important event in the history of NASCAR.

In his home state of Indiana, in front of 300,000 screaming fans at the historic Indianapolis Motor Speedway, Jeff took the checkered flag in the Brickyard 400—the very first NASCAR race run at the world's most famous racetrack.

"Oh my God!" Jeff shouted to his crew over the radio at the finish. "I did it! I did it!"

Just three days after turning 23, Jeff outdueled superstar Ernie Irvan and his No. 36 Pontiac, who had to pit four laps from the end of the 160-lap race because of a flat tire. The two fierce competitors had waged NASCAR war for 20 laps or more, nearly touching bumpers as they roared around the 2.5-mile track as fans watched the high-speed duel.

When Irvan, who recently retired, went to the

pits with his flat tire, Jeff saw his opening and led Brett Bodine to the finish line. He won by .53 seconds, a pretty fair margin by NASCAR measure.

"Me and Ernie were really working on each other," Jeff said when it was all over. "I drove as hard as I could. If he hadn't had the flat, we probably would have come across the finish line side-by-side. Our cars were very equal."

Jeff earned $613,000 that day. But the money isn't what NASCAR fans and insiders were buzzing about after the Indianapolis race. Nor were they comparing notes about how Jeff averaged 131.931 miles per hour despite several cautions for trouble on the track.

What they were talking about that day back in 1994 was what they talk about today. The youngster from Indiana won his first two races at two of the sport's most famous tracks—Charlotte, then Indianapolis. He's an athlete who obviously saves his very best for the very big moments.

"He's got a knack for winning the big races," said veteran sportswriter Bob Myers of Charlotte. "He's just so talented, probably above everybody on the circuit."

After Charlotte and Indianapolis, it was Jeff's knack for the sensational that had people talking.

That, and his tears of joy at Charlotte, had opened the eyes of the sports world.

And he was only just beginning!

Jeff holds up his trophy after winning the 1994 Coca-Cola 600. (Charlotte Observer/Christopher A. Record)

Superstardom!

Jeff was a superstar all right, but he was a superstar who had hit a bump in the road. On an unseasonably warm October Sunday afternoon in 1999, Jeff Gordon came into Martinsville Speedway in the beautiful Blue Ridge Mountains of Virginia as NASCAR's best-known driver. Not only had he won three Winston Cup points championship and countless races, but he was also a handsome and popular spokesman

Jeff looks a bit baffled as he talks with his crew chief, Ray Evernham, after he had to drop out of the Goodwrench 400 1996. (Charlotte Observer/Alan Marler)

for the sport. He was at home on the track, but also as a guest on the David Letterman show late-night on CBS-TV.

He has made millions endorsing ice cream, milk, soft drinks, toothpaste and those sunglasses he always wears. He has also made millions of friends and fans by speaking out about the importance of family and faith. His wife, Brooke, a former beauty queen, is nearly as famous and photographed as him.

But not everything has always gone his way.

In February 1998 at the Bud Shootout at Daytona, Rusty Wallace blew past Jeff on a restart to take the race. Jeff complained about the restart, but the results were upheld—he finished 14th in the field of 17 racers. Then in May 1998 at the prestigious all-star exhibition known as The Winston, Jeff ran out of gas on the final lap and Mark Martin sped home for the win in Charlotte.

But past challenges and disappointments

weren't nearly as big as the latest hurdle that awaited Jeff in the high-speed, split-second world of NASCAR, where one mistake can cost you a race or even your life.

Superstar crew chief Ray Evernham had resigned from the Hendrick team's Rainbow Warriors to form his own team. Brian Whitesell had been promoted to run the race team as crew chief. Everyone in the race world was looking at Jeff's team in turmoil and wondering:

Could Jeff Gordon could keep on winning without the talented, super-organized Evernham?

For Jeff and all his fans, the answer came on their first Sunday as a team, in front of 81,000 screaming fans in Martinsville.

Yes!

When all the other cars on the lead lap went to pit row for new tires during a caution late in the race, Jeff stayed on the track—a move that outfoxed the competition and won him the NAPA 500.

He had to hold off a late charge by the legendary Dale Earnhardt in his famous and fast No. 3 Chevy, to get the dramatic victory. But he got it.

An example of his modesty, Jeff gave Whitesell all the credit.

"It was a great call," Jeff gushed afterward. "He (Brian) said we ought to stay out. I looked around to see what the other guys were going to do. Even though I knew they were coming in, I think it was the right call. It just worked out perfectly."

Whitesell gave the credit right back to his young driver.

"Jeff makes a decision like that easy to make. You have to go for the track position. We knew if we got back in the pack it was not going to be a good thing. We had nothing to lose. We'd either win the race or finish about fifth."

It's the kind of thing Jeff has been doing since

Jeff sits on pit road as his crew works on his #24 DuPont Chevy because of a power steering problem. (Charlotte Observer/Patrick Schneider)

he burst onto the NASCAR scene like a shot in the dark since winning Maxx Race Cards Rookie of the Year in 1993.

Maybe his greatest skill as a driver is that he can find so many different ways to win a race. One day he might have the fastest car set up just right for a certain track and simply outrace everyone to the checkered flag. Another he might avoid a wreck that would strike a less skilled driver and outmanuever a faster foe to the finish line. Or, on another race day, his team would make the right call in the pits—two tires here, a splash of gas there—and he'd outfox the competition. Or he'd rely on what every superstar needs at some point in his career—luck!

He won the Winston Cup championship in 1995, with seven wins, eight poles for being the top qualifier in time trials and more than $4.3 million in earnings. At age 24, he was the youngest season champion ever!

He won 10 races in 1996 and finished second in the points standings by just 37 points to Hendrick teammate Terry Labonte.

He won the Winston Cup championship and 10 victories in 1997, including the biggest one of them all—the legendary Daytona 500 to open the NASCAR season on Feb. 16, 1997.

In a season that might never be topped, he won the points title again in 1998, along with a record 13 victories (including four in a row), seven poles and more than $9 million in race earnings.

He opened the 1999 season with a thrilling win over Rusty Wallace at Daytona, passing him on a daring move with just 11 laps to go. It was one of the seven races he won in 1999—for the fifth straight year, he had the most wins of any driver.

Some fans boo him because he wins so much or because he didn't grow up in the South like so many drivers. NASCAR fans are some of the loudest, most loyal, most demanding in all of sports, and Jeff hasn't quite won all of them over yet.

But others cheer his talent and his dedication, including another NASCAR winner.

"I am, in a lot of ways, a Jeff Gordon fan," Mark Martin told *Sports Illustrated* for a 1998 story. "I approve of him, the way he lives his life, the way he conducts himself, and everything else. If the fans who don't like Jeff Gordon—if they think they don't like him, well, they should just imagine how a different personality could be in his situation. It hurts me to hear him booed because he's good."

For all of Jeff's victories, though, one stands out above all the others.

There were few boos that Monday afternoon of Oct. 11, 1999, when Jeff captured the UAW-GM 500 at Lowe's Motor Speedway. That's because he won the race in front of team owner Rick

Jeff stands on top of his transporter watching qualifying for the 1998 NAPA AutoCare 500. (Charlotte Observer/Jeff Siner)

Hendrick, who was back at the track after winning his battle with leukemia. The medicine he was taking to fight the cancer had sapped his strength. They're like father and son, and when Jeff won in Hendrick's hometown of Charlotte, they both welled up with tears.

"I've been waiting for this day for a long time, waiting to get Rick Hendrick back to Victory Lane," Jeff told the army of reporters waiting for him after the race. "I knew it was going to happen. I just didn't know when."

It's funny how things worked out. The race was rained out Sunday, a dreary, drizzly day when Hendrick didn't feel well enough to make it to the track. But he felt better the next day, a bright and sunny one, and he was there for the dramatic win.

Jeff started the race from the 22nd position after a poor qualifying run. But he kept creeping up and weaving through slower traffic, taking the lead for good from pole-sitter Bobby Labonte's No. 18 Pontiac on the 327th of 334 laps. When Jeff roared out of the pits ahead of third-place finisher Mike Skinner's Chevy near the end, there was no stopping the rainbow-colored No. 24 car.

It was Jeff's fourth win at prestigious Charlotte, and one he believes was somehow planned.

"The way it was all coming down at the end of the race, there are certain times and certain things that happen that you feel like you're not really in control of, that somebody else is," Jeff said that day. "For me to be able to take Rick Hendrick to Victory Lane today was very emotional and probably one of the highlights not only of this year, but of my career."

The headline in *The Charlotte Observer* the next day said it all: "Rainbow Reign."

Not even winning at Charlotte in front of his team owner, though, was the highlight of 1999.

The highlight of Jeff's year came off the track, with a pen instead of a race car at his control.

He signed a lifetime contract to drive for his friend and his team owner, Rick Hendrick! The competition was going to have to deal with Jeff and his Rainbow Warriors well into the new century!

"It's one of the happiest days of my career and one of the happiest days of my life," Jeff said.

Jeff and his wife, Brooke, enjoy a laugh with friends prior to the the running of the 1998 ACDelco 400 at North Carolina Speedway. (Charlotte Observer/Jeff Siner)

Family, Fans, Faith

More than 1,000 NASCAR fans turned out to see Jeff Gordon one beautiful night in Charlotte, N.C., but they didn't come to see him roar around a speedway or win a race.

On NASCAR Family Night at Calvary Church, they came to get his autograph, shake his hand and hear him talk about three most important things in his life:

- His love of family.

- His appreciation for his fans.

- His devotion to a faith he says never deserts him, win or lose.

Life, he told the crowd gathered on the lawn of the big church with the beautiful glass spires, isn't about winning races or being on TV or being recognized wherever you go.

"It's about how can you shine in God's eyes," Jeff said.

Lots of NASCAR drivers are serious about their religious faith. They attend chapel services at the track before each race. They are involved with Motor Racing Outreach, which holds Bible study in race team shops and is there whenever a driver faces a difficult time on or off the track.

Some drivers, like veteran superstar Darrell Waltrip, race around the track with a Bible verse that their wives have taped to their dashboard. Jeff is one of them.

No driver, though, has put his fame and talent to better use than Gordon. To the thousands who follow his career and cheer him on, he's a role model for all that is right.

Whenever he wins a race—and he's won 49 so far to put him in the Top 10 in the history of Winston Cup at the age of 28—he gives credit first to his team. Posters at the Hendrick Motorsports shop near Charlotte emphasize that point. "Together Everyone Achieves More," declares one. Put the first letters together and what does it spell?

T-E-A-M.

Whenever he speaks to reporters or fans, he emphasizes how his family means everything to him.

His mother and stepdad, Carol and John Bickford, helped get him into racing as a youngster

Jeff checks out his car on pit road Saturday as he waits for his chance to qualify for the 1997 Daytona 500 pole. (Charlotte Observer/Jeff Siner)

in California and then Indiana. "I owe my whole career to John and my mom," he told veteran sportswriter Bob Myers. "I wouldn't be a race car driver if not for John, and mom made a lot of sacrifices, too. My parents were my role models and set a lot of examples."

His stepdad even taught him to race clean—as a youngster, Jeff had to give back the winner's trophy if he bumped another car during a race!

Jeff's wife, the former Brooke Sealey of Winston-Salem, N.C., helped inspire him to dedicate his life to God when they were married in 1994.

"I wasn't the neatest kid growing up," he admitted to the Calvary Church crowd, recalling how he was selfish and how he hardly ever read the Bible or went to church.

All that changed after he met Brooke, who was one of the Miss Winston beauty queens at the

NASCAR races, in 1992. Drivers weren't allowed to date Miss Winstons, so the two had to keep their romance secret. One night in Atlanta, they were together when they ran into NASCAR driver Kyle Petty at a Hard Rock Cafe. Their secret was almost found out!

Jeff and Brooke were married in a fancy ceremony in a big hall in downtown Charlotte. They even had a seven-foot-high wedding cake. Now he's a regular church-goer. He has done many TV, radio and newspaper ads for religious causes, including one that appeared in *Parade* magazine. It featured a full-page photo of Jeff with these words: "Through victory and defeat, my relationship with God always keeps me on track."

The ad that appeared in *Reader's Digest* went even deeper: "When you're flying around a track at 180 mph," Jeff said, "danger is always there beside you. But in every race I've ever run, in spite of the danger, I've never been afraid. Because deep inside me there's something greater than fear driving me —and that's my personal relationship with God."

One race weekend during the summer of 1996, Jeff left Michigan Speedway in Brooklyn, Mich., after qualifying for the race and flew to Charlotte just so he could speak to 50,000 men attending a Christian rally at the speedway.

"Flying four hours to do 10 minutes of testimony is quite a tribute to his eagerness to proclaim his faith," said Lowe's Motor Speedway's Jerry Gappens.

Now Brooke goes wherever Jeff goes; they're the most recognized couple in motorsports, maybe in all of sports. She was there at Calvary Church, watching Jeff sign autographs and encourage people to sign up to be a match for cancer patients who

Jeff and Mark Martin's cars sit at the end of pit road as others sit lined up behind them prior to the start of practice for the 1998 NAPA AutoCare 500. (Charlotte Observer/Jeff Siner)

might need a bone marrow transplant. Jeff's interest in that area comes from the fact that his team owner, Rick Hendrick, has been battling leukemia.

As she watched Jeff relate to fans of all ages, Brooke recalled one of the highlights of their time together—meeting evangelist Billy Graham the weekend in 1998 that Jeff spoke at one of Graham's famous crusades at the Hoosier Dome in Indianapolis—Jeff's home state. She still remembers how the sound from the P.A. system echoed off the walls of the huge indoor stadium.

When they're not at the track or meeting fans, Jeff and Brooke often pursue another love of theirs —they're both big movie buffs, and Jeff loves "Seinfeld" and "Melrose Place" on TV!

Watching Jeff smile and chat and hand out autographs as fast as he drives a car makes it easy to see why he is so good at putting the public at ease.

Jeff addresses the media in the winners circle after he took the pole for the Coca Cola 600 race at Charlotte Motor Speedway. (Charlotte Observer/Patrick Schneider)

He said he learned that from one of the best—NBA superstar Charles Barkley. After a game in Phoenix, when Barkley starred for the Suns, Jeff went to meet him.

"He was so friendly," Jeff recalled. "I couldn't believe how he was. That woke me up to what a difference a few minutes with a person can make.

"What Barkley did for us, that made me understand what fans go through when they see me," Jeff says. "They don't want to wait. They get nervous. They worry they may not see you again."

Sometime after that, Jeff and Brooke were eating at a pizza restaurant near Charlotte on a Sunday night after a race. A little girl came in, spotted him, picked up an empty pizza box and asked him to sign it. At Brooke's encouragement, he interrupted his dinner and gave the girl an autograph!

Jeff is always ready to try to encourage those

less fortunate. He visited Brenner Children's Hospital in Winston-Salem one day, and it was obvious from his comments afterward that Jeff realizes that his life should be about more than just winning races and trophies.

"It's very heartbreaking because here you are living a life that couldn't get any better and you're seeing somebody whose life almost couldn't get any worse," he said. "If there is any way I can help, if there is anything I can do, if it's inspiration to somebody because he or she is a fan of mine, that's the easiest thing I could ever do."

On the night with the fans at Calvary, Jeff signed a door panel from one of his wrecked cars. NASCAR lover Greg Faulk, 35, of Matthews, N.C., had bought the panel for $1,500.

Faulk loves the way Jeff uses his head on the track to find the best part of the speedway to run on, and how Jeff knows just when to go to the pits for gas and tires. It doesn't hurt that Jeff races for one of the wealthiest and most organized teams, which keeps him in the best equipment.

"He can take 50 laps to figure out what's wrong with a race car," Faulk said. "It takes some drivers a whole career to figure out one race."

Faulk also loves how Jeff carries himself off the track: "He's a good role model for the kids. He's just too good. He has struck my heart."

After signing autographs for more than an hour —car parts, posters, photographs, sneakers, model No. 24 cars, caps and more—Jeff posed for some pictures. Every time a youngster nervously shuffled beside him, Jeff would put his arm around the fan, whisper a few comforting words, then smile for the camera for what must have been the millionth time. Everyone seemed at ease.

Jeff graciously signs autographs for fans after taking the pole for the 1998 Coca-Cola 600 race at Charlotte Motor Speedway. (Charlotte Observer/Jeff Siner)

When the autograph session was over, Jeff went out to the church lawn. He was wearing his customary knit shirt and tennis shoes. Informally dressed, at 5 feet 7 inches tall and just 150 pounds, he fit in with the young crowd.

He could be one of the kids, if he wasn't superstar Jeff Gordon!

Under the stars on a clear night, Jeff climbed the stage, accepted the applause of the crowd and shared the story of all that he has—a loving wife, a loyal family, a strong faith and a great race team—and all that it has made him on and off the track.

A champion!

Said Jeff to the crowd: "I've been very, very blessed."

"Ricki" Hendrick IV and Jeff both drive #24 sponsored by DuPont Automotive Finishes. (Charlotte Observer/Gayle Shomer)

CHAPTER FIVE

Roaring into the Future

S ometimes a champion doesn't show his best stuff in victory.

Sometimes a champion shows what he's really made of in defeat.

Jeff Gordon finished a disappointing 38th in the final race of the 1999 NASCAR season at Atlanta Motor Speedway, going out after 181 laps with a blown engine. Bobby Labonte won for the powerful Joe Gibbs race team, and 1999 Winston Cup champion Dale Jarrett finished second.

Jeff races under the checkered flag to win the 1998 ACDelco 400 and Winston Cup points championship. (Charlotte Observer/ Jeff Siner)

But instead of making excuses or blaming someone else for the problem, Jeff chose instead to look ahead and promise to work even harder.

Even though he won seven races in 1999—more than any other driver on the Winston Cup circuit—Jeff said, "I'm looking forward to the off-season to get this team back on track. We've got to make a lot of adjustments over the off-season because we lost our pit crew and Ray (Evernham) and a couple of other guys. We weren't really prepared for this at the end of the season. If you're not perfect, you're not going to be able to win races."

Perfection.

It's what a determined Jeff is after in the 2000 season that begins Feb. 20 at the legendary Daytona 500 on the sunny east coast of central Florida. It's what he's after every time he climbs into Hendrick Motorsports' Chevrolet. It's what folks around

NASCAR think he's got a chance to reach in the years to come.

"He's already won more races than Richard Petty, A.J. Foyt and Mario Andretti at this age (Jeff is 28)," said Lowe's Motor Speedway President Humpy Wheeler, one of the most respected men in the sport. "He's really got the potential of becoming one of the top race car drivers in motorsports. He's already got a step up on most drivers."

Just look at the record:

Going into the 2000 season, Jeff ranks 10th in all-time Winston Cup wins with 49, tied with Rusty Wallace.

He has won the most races for each of the past five seasons. His super 1999 season came despite his crew chief, Ray Evernham, and five members of his famed Rainbow Warriors pit crew leaving for other teams. The crewmen finished out the season, then left. Evernham left in midseason—it was one of the biggest stories of the 1999 NASCAR year. After the season, the crew chief chosen to succeed Evernham—Brian Whitesell—was promoted to team manager and will oversee the overall race operation. Jeff's new crew chief is Robbie Loomis, who comes over from the famed Petty Enterprises.

Jeff is optimistic: "The team will be competitive."

Jeff tied with Mark Martin for the most poles won in the 1990s—30 times, they each ran the fastest in qualifying to earn the right to begin a race in first place.

His overall winnings since he first stepped onto a Winston Cup track, Nov. 15, 1992, at the Hooters 500 at Atlanta Motor Speedway stands at a whopping $31 million.

No wonder Wheeler ticks off all the reasons he believes Jeff is a superstar who, barring an injury

A Winston Cup official stands in front of Jeff's car with his hands on his hips enforcing a one lap penalty on him for overshooting his pit during the 1999 Bud Shootout at Daytona International Speedway. (Charlotte Observer/Jeff Siner)

on the track or something you can't possibly predict off it, has what it takes to keep that status.

He's got experience racing and winning, Wheeler said, starting when he was four years old on his BMX bicycle in California.

He's got amazing eyesight that helps him spot problems a split-second before the next driver—a great gift when you're going 200 miles per hour at Talladega!

He's got a calm, even personality, which you need when you're in a four-hour race in the heat of summer in front of 200,000 screaming fans. "Getting emotional in a race car isn't the thing to do," Wheeler said, noting how hard it is to be a NASCAR driver: Look up in the stands or think about something other than the race for even one split second and you're in deep trouble!

"There's no other athlete who has to focus on one thing and one thing alone for more than two

Jeff whoops it up in Victory Lane after winning the Daytona 500 1997. (Charlotte Observer/Jeff Siner)

hours," Wheeler said.

Jeff is a clean-living man with a strong religious faith who doesn't drink or let anything else get in the way of going all-out to win.

And on the Saturday nights and Sunday afternoons when he doesn't win, he has his wife, Brooke, to support him. NASCAR is one of the few sports where all except one athlete goes home a loser.

"I have never known a great race car driver without a great wife," Wheeler said. "Somebody's got to pick them up. It's not the buddies, it's not the team. It's the wife."

With a new TV deal for 2001 putting NASCAR on NBC and Fox most every weekend, Wheeler believes Jeff also has the good looks and winning personality to remain a great ambassador for the sport.

"It will expand his presence, not only in the United States but the world," Wheeler said. "His

Jeff does "donuts" at the Start/Finish line at the conclusion of the NAPA 500. Gordon won the 1995 Winston Cup championship during the race. (Charlotte Observer/Mark B. Sluder)

picture will be on the cover of *Time* magazine instead of *Sports Illustrated*."

He also believes Jeff will benefit from what all great athletes must have—a great rival to push them on to even more sensational heights. Larry Bird had Magic Johnson in the NBA. Richard Petty had Junior Johnson in NASCAR. Home run champion Mark McGwire has Sammy Sosa in baseball. It looks like Jeff is going to get his stiffest challenge in the years to come from rising superstars Tony Stewart and Dale Earnhardt Jr.

Who knows whether Jeff can ever reach the amazing mark set by the greatest NASCAR superstar of them all—Richard "The King" Petty and his 200 victories and seven Winston Cup championships in 1,185 starts.

Petty had 50 races during some years in setting his mark; the men of NASCAR today only drive 30 to 35 races a year. So it might be tough for anyone to do what Petty has done.

But as you put on your NASCAR cap and shirt this season to cheer on Jeff or some other daring driver, think about this: Richard Petty ended his NASCAR career at the Hooters 500 in Atlanta on Nov. 15, 1992. That was the same day and race that Jeff Gordon began his NASCAR career, finishing 31st and showing the world just a glimpse of what he was about to do.

One legend said goodbye and another said hello on the same day!

"That seems like a long time ago," he says, "but at the same time I can't believe all that has happened."

What happened that day at the speedway outside Atlanta is that a legend in the making began racing for the checkered flag in the greatest racing league of them all.

The young legend is still racing for the checkered flag, and now he's winning.

That isn't about to stop.

As Humpy Wheeler says for fans everywhere: "I think Jeff's just going to keep rolling on."

Jeff Gordon Quick Facts

Birthdate: Aug. 4, 1971.

Birthplace: Vallejo, Calif.

Where he grew up: Pittsboro, Ind.

Home: Florida, though he also has a residence in the Charlotte (N.C.) area. He prefers not to get too specific, so he can keep some privacy away from the track!

Height: 5 feet 7 inches.

Weight: 150.

Family: He and wife, Brooke, married on Thanksgiving weekend 1994 in Charlotte.

Fan club: 20,000 members.

Hobbies: He and Brooke love watching movies.

What he wears: Blue jeans, knit shirt and tennis shoes whenever possible.

Race team: Hendrick Motorsports.

Race team nickname: Rainbow Warriors.

Shop location: Harrisburg, N.C.

Jeff celebrates with crew chief Ray Evernham as his car is pushed into the NASCAR inspecion area after winning the pole position in a 1994 race. (Charlotte Observer/Mark B. Sluder)

Jeff Gordon Career Highlights

• Forty-nine career wins, starting with the Coca-Cola 600 at Charlotte Motor Speedway (now Lowe's Motor Speedway) on May 29, 1994.

• Career Winston Cup race earnings of $31,290,407.

• Career poles: 30, good for 20th best in the history of Winston Cup.

• Most wins each of the last five seasons: 7 in 1995, 10 in 1996, 10 in 1997, 13 in 1998 and 7 in 1999.

• Became the youngest Winston Cup champion in 1995 (he was 24) in his third year on tour.

• Won the 1997 and 1998 Winston Cup championships.

• Tied two modern-era records in 1998—13 wins in one season and four wins in a row.

• Youngest driver ever to win the Daytona 500—he was 25 when he captured the famed race on Feb. 16, 1997.

• Won the inaugural Brickyard 400 at legendary Indianapolis Motor Speedway, on Aug. 6, 1994.

• Was 1993 Maxx Race Cards Rookie of the Year in the Winston Cup series.

Jeff Gordon's 1999 Wins

• Daytona 500, Daytona International Speedway, Feb. 14.

• Cracker Barrel 500, Atlanta Motor Speedway, March 14.

• California 500, California Speedway, May 2.

• Save Mart/Kragen 350, Sears Point Raceway, June 27.

• Frontier at the Glen, Watkins Glen International, Aug. 15.

• NAPA 500, Martinsville Speedway, Oct. 3

• UAW-GM 500, Lowe's Motor Speedway, Oct. 11.

Jeff gets sprayed down with champagne by teammates Terry Labonte and Ricky Craven following his victory in the 1997 Daytona 500. (Charlotte Observer/Jeff Siner)

NASCAR's All-Time Winners

Richard Petty 200

David Pearson 105

Bobby Allison 84

Darrell Waltrip 84

Cale Yarborough 83

Dale Earnhardt 71

Lee Petty 54

Ned Jarrett 50

Junior Johnson 50

Jeff Gordon 49

Rusty Wallace 49

Jeff sits in his car on pit road at Daytona International Speedway, waiting for the start of the Bud Shootout. (Charlotte Observer/Jeff Siner)

Jeff Gordon's Ride

Team: Hendrick Motorsports.

Owner: Rick Hendrick.

Car number: 24.

Make: Chevrolet Monte Carlo.

Sponsor: DuPont Automotive Finishes.

Colors: Red and blue, trimmed in yellow and green.

Crew chief: Robbie Loomis.

Engine: Chevrolet V-8 SB 2.

Transmission: 4-speed GM manual.

Fuel system: 22 gallons.

Weight: 3,400 pounds.

Horsepower: 700@8000 rpm.

Thoughts at the Finish Line

"I think he's just going to keep rolling on."

– Lowe's Motor Speedway President Humpy Wheeler,
  on Jeff Gordon.

"I've been very, very blessed."

– Jeff Gordon.

Baseball Superstar Series Titles

Collect Them All!

___ Mark McGwire: Mac Attack!

___ #1 *Derek Jeter: The Yankee Kid*

___ #2 *Ken Griffey Jr.: The Home Run Kid*

___ #3 *Randy Johnson: Arizona Heat!*

___ #4 *Sammy Sosa: Slammin' Sammy*

___ #5 *Bernie Williams: Quiet Superstar*

___ #6 *Omar Vizquel: The Man with the Golden Glove*

___ #7 *Mo Vaughn: Angel on a Mission*

___ #8 *Pedro Martinez: Throwing Strikes*

___ #9 *Juan Gonzalez: Juan Gone!*

___ #10 *Tony Gwynn: Mr. Padre*

___ #11 *Kevin Brown: Kevin with a "K"*

___ #12 *Mike Piazza: Mike and the Mets*

___ #13 *Larry Walker: Canadian Rocky*

___ #14 *Nomar Garciaparra: High 5!*

___ #15 *Sandy and Roberto Alomar: Baseball Brothers*

___ #16 *Mark Grace: Winning with Grace*

___ #17 *Curt Schilling: Phillie Phire!*

___ #18 *Alex Rodriguez: A+ Shortstop*

___ #19 *Roger Clemens: Rocket!*

Only $4.95 per book!

Call Toll Free: 1-877-424-BOOK (2665) or
visit us at www.sportspublishinginc.com

Football Superstar Series Titles
Collect Them All!

Only $4.95 per book!

Basketball Superstar Series Titles
Collect Them All!

____ #1 *Kobe Bryant: The Hollywood Kid*

____ #2 *Keith Van Horn: Nothing But Net*

____ #3 *Antoine Walker: Kentucky Celtic*

____ #4 *Kevin Garnett: Scratching the Surface*

____ #5 *Tim Duncan: Slam Duncan*

____ #6 *Reggie Miller: From Downtown*

____ #7 *Jason Kidd: Rising Sun*

____ #8 *Vince Carter: Air Canada*

Only $4.95 per book!

Call Toll Free: 1-877-424-BOOK (2665) or visit us at www.sportspublishinginc.com

NASCAR Superstar Series Titles

___ #1 *Jeff Gordon: Rewriting the Record Books*

___ #2 *Dale Jarrett: Son of Thunder*

___ #3 *Dale Earnhardt: The Intimidator*

___ #4 *Tony Stewart: Hottest Thing on Wheels*

Hockey Superstar Series Titles

___ #1 *John LeClair: Flying High*

___ #2 *Mike Richter: Gotham Goalie*

___ #3 *Paul Kariya: Maine Man*

___ #4 *Dominik Hasek: The Dominator*

___ #5 *Jaromir Jagr: Czechmate*

___ #6 *Martin Brodeur: Picture Perfect*

___ #8 *Ray Bourque: Bruins Legend*

Only $4.95 per book!

Collect Them All!